Is God my Imaginary Friend?

Written by
C.C Strachan

Illustrated by
Chernelle Walkes

ISBN-13: 978-0692435168

DEDICATION

This book is dedicated to my wonderful son Anton Carl Strachan Jr and to my nieces and nephews.

To my supportive family this book would not have been possible
without your encouragement and to Charlene Carty-Simmons for always believing in me.

And most importantly all thanks and praise to God and His Holy Spirit for His divine inspiration.

ACKNOWLEDGMENTS

To my amazing husband Anton and my niece Chernelle, thank you both for using your talents in making this book a reality.

Why should I talk to Jesus daddy?
He's not like raggy or teddy,
I can't see him anywhere,
or do I make believe he is here?

My little one,
just because Jesus can't be seen,
doesn't mean He isn't real.
Your five senses can tell you much
but some things are just a hunch.

Can you touch your little toesy,
and smell with your nosy?

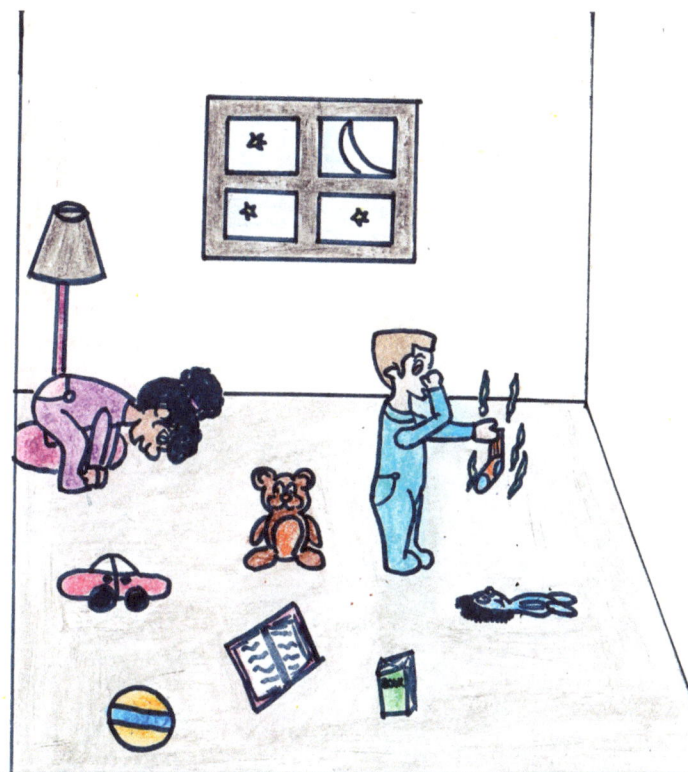

Do you like smelling stinky socks? Oh Yuck!
No one likes smelling stinky socks.

How about tasting
your favorite ice-cream?

I bet your tummy
says yummy!

Now let's scream.

Now stop please.

How did you hear?

With your toes or your ear? (*your ear*)

Can you see birds fly,
way up in the sky?

For we feel with our fingers
and smell with our noses.
We taste with our mouth
and use it to shout!

We see with our eyes,
even using it to cry.

But what about the things we do not see.

Like the air we breathe,

do you think it's real?

Hmm, let's see.

For the air we breathe is as real
as you and me. You can tell by watching
the birds and the bees.

For they fly through the air
since there's no traffic there.

So now you know my little one,
that you just must not shun
things you can't see
and think they're not real.

But wait, we're not done.

What about music? Let's try this one for fun.

So put on your thinking cap
and let's begin to clap.
Did you hear a sound,
as you clap along?

Boogy Boogy oui! (pronounced wee)

Absolutely!

Did you see the sound
as it moved along,
from your hands to your ear
so that you can hear?

Boogy Boogy nay.

No oh way!

So now you know the big reveal:

that some things *not* seen are still real!

Like God who is real as the air we breathe
and the love between you and me.
He loves it when you call His name
and shout Hallelujah with no shame.

So remember God when you see
birds and bees flying free.

And remember God when you can't see
the air in which we all breathe.

For we are the works of His hand
and in it, we all stand.

So now I'll ask you to pray:

Dear Jesus,
Now I know you're real
And I hope to always feel
You in my heart,
So that we can never be apart.
And teach me always to do right
And to love you with all my might
And Jesus, help my friends to see
Just how real you can be.
Amen.

ABOUT THE AUTHOR

C. C. Strachan has been a Christian for over fifteen years and lives in Brooklyn, New York, with her Evangelist husband and their four-year-old son. She holds a master's degree in financial engineering and has worked in the financial industry for over fifteen years; she's presently pursuing an additional master's degree in Christian apologetics from Biola University. C.C. Strachan and her husband are the founders of Power of Worship Ministries, Inc., a nonprofit organization that provides food for the homeless.

In the mythical world of AbbaLand, all the letters live in harmony with their creator, Abba. A and E, however, will conspire to exile one letter out of AbbaLand forever!

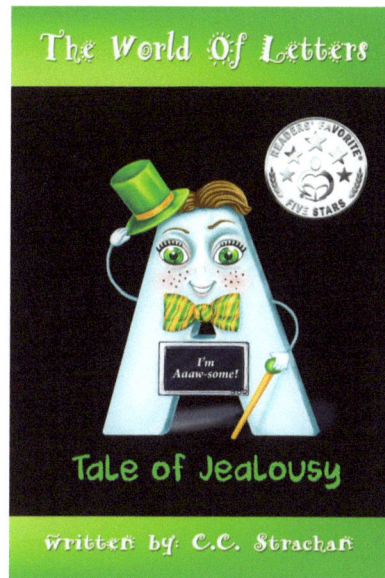

Look for other C.C. Strachan books at:

www.powkids.org